COURTHOUSE INDEXES ILLUSTRATED

ABOUT THE AUTHOR

Christine Rose, CG, CGL, FASG, is a Certified Genealogist, a Certified Genealogical Lecturer, and a full-time professional genealogist. She was elected Fellow, American Society of Genealogists, an honor bestowed by peers based on quantity and quality of publications, and limited to only fifty at any time. She was the recipient of the prestigious Donald Lines Jacobus award for two genealogy books. Compiler of numerous genealogies and articles; an Associate of the Board for Certification of Genealogists; former Vice President of Association of Professional Genealogists and of the Federation of Genealogical Societies, and a long-time columnist for the latter's *Forum* have all contributed to a productive career in the field of genealogy. Christine, well known as a lecturer, has presented at national and regional conferences, at the National Institute of Historical Research in Washington, D.C., and is on the faculty of the Samford University Institute of Genealogy and Historical Research in Birmingham. She is also founder of the Rose Family Association and its editor since its inception. Her articles have appeared in a number of the national journals and magazines. As an author, her books include the highly praised *Courthouse Research for Family Historians: Your Guide to Genealogical Treasures; Genealogical Proof Standard: Building a Solid Case; Nicknames: Past & Present; Family Association, Organization and Management*; and others. She is also co-author of the high-seller, *The Complete Idiot's Guide to Genealogy.*

COURTHOUSE INDEXES ILLUSTRATED

By

CHRISTINE ROSE, CG, CGL, FASG

SAN JOSE, CALIFORNIA
2006

COPYRIGHT 2006 BY CHRISTINE ROSE. ALL RIGHTS RESERVED. NO PART MAY BE REPRODUCED IN ANY FORM INCLUDING ELECTRONIC AND INFORMATIONAL STORAGE OR RETRIEVAL SYSTEMS, WITHOUT THE WRITTEN PERMISSION OF THE AUTHOR. THE ONLY EXCEPTION IS FOR BRIEF QUOTES FOR WHICH PERMISSION IS GRANTED PROVIDED CREDIT IS GIVEN.

ISBN 0-929626-17-6

FIRST PRINTING 2006
10 9 8 7 6 5 4 3 2 1

PUBLISHED BY: CRPUBLICATIONS, 1474 MONTELEGRE DR., SAN JOSE, CA 95120

PRINTED BY THOMSON SHORE, INC., DEXTER, MICHIGAN
AUTHOR'S EMAIL: CHRISTINE4ROSE@CS.COM
AUTHOR'S WEBSITE: WWW.CHRISTINE4ROSE.COM

COVER DESIGN BY ANN SILBERLICHT OF SILBERLICHT STUDIO

Dedicated to every researcher who follows the trail to the wonderful world of courthouse records.

Other Books by this Author
Courthouse Research for Family Historians
Genealogical Proof Standard
Nicknames: Past and Present
Military Pension Laws 1776-1858
Family Associations: Organization and Management
The Brothers Rev. Robert Rose and Rev. Charles Rose
Robert Rose of Connecticut Who Came in 1634
Rose War Files: Vol. I
Rose War Files: Vol. II
Frederick Rose of Virginia, North Carolina and Tennessee
Andrew Rose of Mercer County, Pennsylvania
Abstracts of Virginia Rose Estates Prior to 1800
Ancestors and Descendants of Anson Parmilee Stone
David Christian Crummey Family
Declarations of Intention Santa Clara Co., Calif. 1850-1870

Co-author of
The Complete Idiot's Guide to Genealogy

CONTENTS

LIST OF ILLUSTRATIONS X
INTRODUCTION XI

CHAPTER 1: COTT INDEXES 1
CHAPTER 2: RUSSELL INDEX 15
CHAPTER 3: GRAVES INDEX 23
CHAPTER 4: PROCEEDINGS INDEX 25
CHAPTER 5: CAMPBELL INDEX 29
CHAPTER 6: VOWEL INDEX 33
CHAPTER 7: STARK INDEX 37
CHAPTER 8: DEVISOR/DEVISEE INDEX 39
CHAPTER 9: TRADITIONAL INDEXES 41
CHAPTER 10: AND OTHERS 45

INDEX 57

ILLUSTRATIONS

Figure

1-1	Cott: initial two letters	1
1-2	Cott: initial two letter fuller illustration	3
1-3	Cott: initial letters by two or three letters	5
1-4	Cott: Family Name Index, Sub-index	7
1-5	Cott: Family Name Index, Sub-index	8
1-6	Cott: Family Name Index, Main Index	9
1-7	Cott: initial two letters variation	11
1-8	Cottco: Universal index top of page	12
1-9	Cottco: Universal index bottom of page	12
1-10	Paul Co. index	13
2-1	Russell: Key Index	17
2-2	Russell: Key Index break-out of names	18
2-3	Russell: Key Index variation	21
3-1	Graves: Tabular Initial Index	24
4-1	Estate index cover/Proceedings Cover	25
4-2	Estate Index leading to Proceedings	26
4-3	Proceedings index/docket	27
5-1	Campbell: first name index	30
6-1:	Vowel index	35
6-2	Vowel index: 2nd part (item)	36
7-1	Stark index	38
8-1	Devisee index	40
9-1	Traditional index	43
10-1	Division by letters of surname and given name	46
10-2	Variation of first three letters of surname	47
10-3	Subdividing given names	48
10-4	Bollman's index	50
10-5	Orphan's Court	52
10-6	Town Hall index	53
10-7	Variation of initial letter of surname and given name	54
10-8	Civil Court index (Judgements)	55
10-9	Hustings Court Index Book cover	56

INTRODUCTION

My book *Courthouse Research for Family Historians* (San Jose, Calif.: CR Publications, 2004) explained in detail the myriad indexes found in courthouses across America. This present book, *Courthouse Indexes Illustrated* is not meant to supplant that information, but is intended to illustrate the indexes and give step-by-step instructions on how to use them to find the names sought.

There are so many variations of indexes. Most are simple, some are complicated. One thing seems likely—all of us at one time or another have missed records because we did not understand the index we were using. It is my hope that by studying these illustrations, and keeping this book handy as you research in the courthouse or in microfilm, that this guide will assist you in finding all the entries for your family.

You'll find that a search example may give steps to find a specific name, while the description with the illustration leads you through a different name. This should broaden your practice. Try to find those on your own, and then compare your result with the one given. You'll readily see which indexes are giving you the most difficulty.

After reading this, it may be a good idea to return to some of those indexes you used years ago, and give them another try. Your family may be in them, afterall!

CR

CHAPTER 1
THE COTT INDEXES

There are a variety of Cott indexes. Some are based on the first two letters of the surname. Some use the first two or three letters plus those with the same sound. Yet another uses two parts and is grouped by sound. There are others, too.

USING THE FIRST TWO LETTERS OF THE SURNAME

The first index mentioned above is illustrated in Figures 1-1 and 1-2. It uses the first two letters of the surname, regardless of what those two letters may be. Looking below, note that all surnames from EP up to EZ fall into the

First two Letters of Surname.			First two Letters of Surname.		
Ep to Ez			**Fa Fe Fi**		
First Letter of Given Name and Page.			First Letter of Given Name and Page.		
A ...76	H ...85	P Q 97	A ..106	H ..115	P Q 127
B ...78	I ...86	R .. 98	B ..108	I ..116	R ..128
C ...79	J ...86	S .. 99	G ..109	J ..116	S ..129
D ...80	K L .92	T ..101	D ..110	K L 122	T ..131
E ...81	M ...93	U V 102	E ..111	M ..123	U V 132
F ...83	N ...96	W ..103	F ..113	N ..126	W ..133
G ...84	O ...96	Y Z 105	G ..114	O ..126	Y Z 135

Figure 1-1. The first two letters of the surname are indicated by the top column. The vertical alphabet represents the first letter of the given name. The name of ALEXANDER EPSON would be on page 76, while THOMAS FENMORE would be on page 131.

first column. Thus, Epson, Erman, Estie, and Exnard would all fall there.

Figure 1-2 is a fuller illustration of Figure 1-1, and is page 17 of the book. (See the page number in the upper left hand corner of Figure 1-2.)

The Search In Figure 1-2

1. If you are searching for IDA EBERLY, start with the surname. Go to the first column "Ea to Ef."

2. Then, for the first or given name, use the divisions listed vertically below that heading. The given name of Ida would be under "I" on page 17.

3. Page 17 is the page shown in the illustration. In this index (as in many others) each page has the chart on top, and listings below. The first few listings are for Ida Eberly.

The first column is "From" (the Grantor), and continues with "To" (the person receiving the action), "Kind of Instrument," Miscel'ns Records Volume and Page," "Date of Instrument," and "Date of Record[ing]." All of these are important to note.[1]

To see the full document, now proceed to the shelves to find the cited volume, and then the page which was cited.

---

1. The illustration in Figure 1-2 is a "Grantor Index to Miscellaneous Records," and thus includes a variety of non-deed documents such as Releases, Powers of Attorney, etc. It is important to seek out any such indexes which may be on the courthouse shelves. Many counties include miscellaneous records in the regular deed indexes (or did in earlier times). But, if the county you are researching did not, those records will be lost to you if you don't seek out the index for those documents. In Figure 1-2, the especially important Powers of Attorney would have been missed.

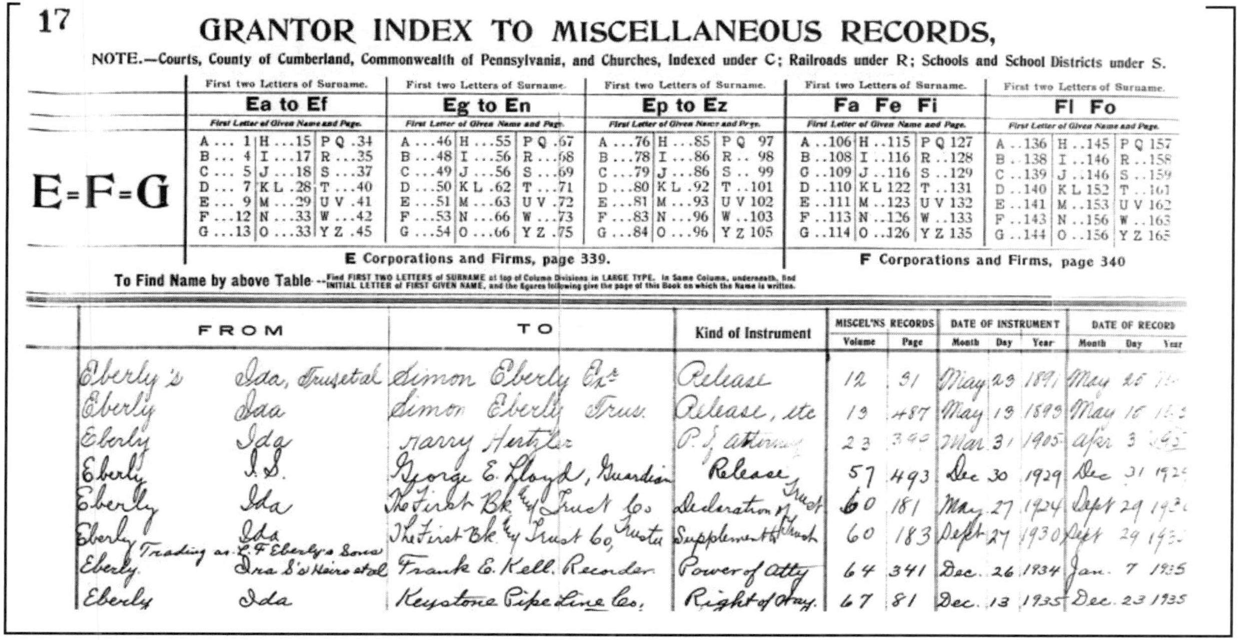

CHAPTER 1: *The Cott Indexes* 3

Figure 1-2. This is a fuller illustration of the same index book page (17) in Figure 1-1. Note that the chart is at the top of the page, and the entries below. Each page would be similarly arranged.

GROUPING BY SOUND

Figure 1-3 is based on the first two or three letters of the surname, instead of just on two. It attempts to group same sounding names, so it may also include a combination of other letters that are similar in that sound. For example, look at the 4th column of Figure 1-3. Surnames starting with Roa to Ron fall into this group, but additionally, Rho has been added because of its sound.

Below the grouping of surname divisions are the categories by given name. Those starting with A (such as Alexander or Arthur) are in the "A B" listings on page 204, those starting with C or D (such as Charles or Daniel) are on p. 209, etc.

THE SEARCH IN FIGURE 1-3

1. Looking for LEMUEL ROANE? Starting with the surname divisions along the top, go to the heading "Roa to Ron Rho."

2. Then look for the first letter of the given name of Lemuel. Those divisions, beneath the main heading, would indicate that L is in the "K L M" division. LEMUEL ROANE (if he appears in the index) will be on page 238.

> **Check the variant spellings of the surname when you use this type of index. Note that in Figure 1-3, Edward Roane would be on page 214, while Edward Roone would be on page 271.**

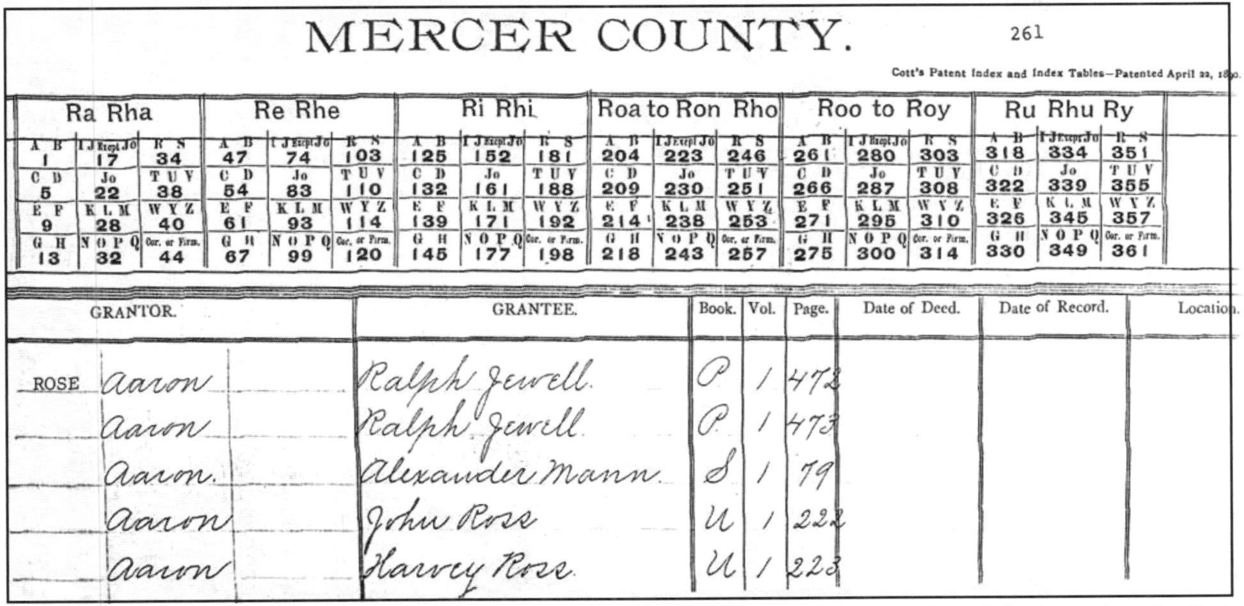

CHAPTER 1: *The Cott Indexes* 5

Figure 1-3. The above version of Cott gives the surname divisions along the top, left to right, based on the first two or three letters of the surname. In some cases other similar sounding combinations are included, such as "Rho" added to "Roa to Ron." Beneath that are divisions by the initial letter of the given name. Be sure to check the variant spellings of the surname when you use this type of index. In the above example, Martha Roice would be in the 4th column, while Martha Royce would be in the 5th column.

FAMILY NAME INDEXES

Cott Family Name indexes consist of two parts, The Sub-Index (Figures 1-4 and 1-5) and The Main Index (see Figure 1-6).

THE SUB-INDEX

First, in the Sub-Index (see illustration in Figure 1-4) names similar in sound but spelled differently are grouped together. As can be seen, WELBORN was entered under the column of "Wel Wil" It was assigned page/section 64. Names that are grouped together by sound may include for example:

Bair-Bare-Baer
Bear-Baehr
Shafer-Schafer
Read-Reed-Reid
Kline-Klein

A surname is only written once, the first time a document is recorded for that surname. It is entered under the proper heading, and assigned a page number. Any further entries for that surname use the same assigned page number.

THE SEARCH IN FIGURE 1-4

1. First find the surname and page/section number in the Sub-Index.

2. Using the page/section number listed with the surname, proceed to the Main Index. (This is usually in the same index book as the Sub-Index, further back in the book. Just be sure to use the Sub-Index first in this two part Family Name indexing system.)

CHAPTER 1: *The Cott Indexes* 7

Wel Wil	Page	Wel—Continued Wil—Continued	Page
WELBORN	64	WELLS	67
WELCH ~~WELDON~~ WELLER	65 66 66	WELSH	68
WELCHEL WELLMAN	66 66-A	WELTER	69
WILBANKS	126	WILLARD	137
WILBERT	126-A 126-A	WILLAMAN	137-A
WILBURN	127	WILLBANKS	138
WILCOX	128	WILLEFORD	139
WILDE	129	WILLEY	140
WILDER	130	WILLIAMS	141
WILDERMUTH	128-A		
WILDMAN	131	WILLIAMSON	142
WILEY	131	WILLIAMSTON	142-A
WILHELM	132	WILLIFORD	143
WILHELMSEN	132-A		
WILHITE	132	WILLIMON	144
WILHOIT	132		
WILKERSON	133	WILLINGHAM	145
WILKES	133	WILLIS	146
WILKEY	133	WILLOUGHBY	146
WILKIE	134	WILLS	147
WILKINS	135	WILLSON	148
		Wilson	148A
WILKINSON	136	WILSON	149

Figure 1-4. The Sub-Index of the Cott Family Name Indexes. The above (explained on the previous page) represents families who had at least one document filed or recorded. Using the number assigned to that surname, proceed to the Main Index (usually in the same index book) to determine the volume and page number where the document will appear.

Some versions of the Sub-Index draw certain surnames together, *even if the initial letter of the surname is different.* For example, see Figure 1-5.

b or d	f or k	l	m	n	p	r	s	t	v x or z and Odd
Baeder	Cook	Bailey	Dempsey	Blaine	Beaupre	Bair	Crosby	Deitz	Baxter
Daubert	Groff	Deihl	Gamble	Donahue	Fippen	Gearhart	Frost	Hyatt	Davis
Kreider	Lakin	Fuller	Krumm	Lynn	Knapp	Myers	Keiser	Layton	Frey
Schwab	Mackey	Haller	McMann	McNally	Lipton	Pearson	Lucas	Metters	McCoy
Weber	Staufer	Wilson	Ramsey	Stein	Seip	Schearer	McChesney	Tetrick	Weaver

Sub-Index Columns Illustrated, with Examples of Names placed in proper Columns

If no letters like those heading the columns appear in name after second letter look for name under Odd. Notice that c g h and the vowels a e i o u w y are not column-letters.

Figure 1-5. In the above Sub-Index note that the classifications group certain names together depending upon letters contained after the second letter of the surname, regardless of initial letter of the surname. If none of the letters across the top appear after the second letter, they fall into the "odd" column. (The name of LOWE, for example, would fall into the "odd" column.) Notice too, in the instructions within the illustration, that certain letters are disregarded.

The Main Index

Once the surname is found in the Sub-Index, use the number assigned to that surname and proceed to the page/section in the Main Index, usually in that same index book. Once you find the entry in the Main index, use the Volume and page shown to locate the actual record book on the courthouse shelves. There you will find the complete document started on the cited page.

Family Names	GRANTEES Given Names A B C D E F G H	Given Names I J K L M N O	Given Names P Q R S T U V W Y Z	GRANTORS	Kind of Instrument	Book	Page
Rose	G F			William & Elendor McClure	Deed	27	370
do		J D		Silas & D M Rose	Deed	27	419
do		J D		W B Lenoir	Deed	28	120
do etal	A J			Silas Rose	Deed	28	208
do	G F			J D & A S Rose	Deed	28	544
do			Winnie L	John H & M J Rose	Deed	29	583
do		M N		Louisa Rose	Deed	29	597

Figure 1-6. This is the Main Index—in this case a General Index to Deeds. As mentioned, the Main Index is the second part of the two part Cott Family Name Index. The surname entries are listed together, (shown as "Family Name" in the far left column). Often the given name is then indexed by three divisions starting with A, B, C, D, E, F, G, and H in the first column; I, J, K, L, M, N, and O in the second column, and P, Q, R, S, T, U, V, W, X, Y, and Z in the third column. The above is a Grantee index. The first entry is G. F. Rose, grantee, from William and Elendor McClure. The second entry is J. D. Rose from Silas and D. M. Rose.

Further Division by Given Name

In a common variation of the Main Index, there is a further subdivision by given name, usually in three columns. Given names starting with A, B, C, D, E, F, G, and H in the first column; I, J, K, L, M, N, and O in the second column, and P, Q, R, S, T, U, V, W, X, Y, and Z in the third column. (See Figure 1-6.).

VARIATIONS

Cott indexes have, it seems, endless variations. In Figure 1-7, again, the first two letters of the surname are listed, but charted and divided a bit differently than the previous illustrations. Ninety-six classications appear in the illustrated chart.

Note the "disclaimer" under the chart which states "There may be a few names which this Key Table does not classify. All such names are indexed with those beginning with X, sheet 95." It would therefore behoove researchers to always check sheet (section) 95 just to be sure their surname is not listed there.

The Search in Figure 1-7

1. For JOSEPH BEHRAIN go to the second column headed by "B."

2. Then proceed to the subdivision beneath which shows "Be 6." This represents the first two letters of the surname. Go to page 6 and those listings, if any, will be there.

CHAPTER 1: *The Cott Indexes* 11

A		B		C		D		E		F		G		H		I-J		K		L	
Aa to Ak	1	Ba	5	Bo	9	Ca	13	Co	16	Da	20	Ea to Ek	24	Fa	28	Ga	32	Ha	36	Ho	39	Ia to Iz	42	Ka	46	La	50
Al	2	Be	6	Br	10	Ce Ch Ci	14	Cr	17	De Di	21	El-m-n-o	25	Fe Fi	29	Ge Gh Gi	33			Hu	40	Ja Je Ji	43	Ke to Ki	47	Le Li	51
Am-n-o-p-q	3	Bi-j	7	Bu	11	Cl	15	Cu	18	Do Dr	22	Ep-q-r-s	26	Fl Fo	30	Gl to Go	34	He	37	Jo	44	Kl Kn Ko.	48	Ll Lo	52
Ar to Az	4	Bl	8	By-z	12			Cy Cz	19	Da-w-y	23	Et to Ez	27	Fr-a-y	31	Gr-u-w-y	35	Hi	38	Hy	41	Ju Jy	45	Kr to Kz	49	Lu Ly	53

There may be a few names which this Key Table does not classify. All such names are indexed with those beginning X; Sheet No. 95

COPYRIGHTED 1952
A-A-207619

REG. U.S. PAT OFFICE *Cott McCott* County Indexes Since 1895 An Identifying Trade Mark

COTT SURNAME KEY TABLE No. 96 © 1952
Made by The Cott Index Company, Columbus, Ohio
Mfg. Cott Patent Index Systems

M		Mc		N-O		P		Q-R		S		T		U-V		W-X-Y-Z	
Ma	54	McA - McB	60	Na Ne Ni	64	Pa	67	Q	71	Sa Se Si	75	So Sp Sq-r	79	Ta	83	Wa	89	Wo	93
Me	55	McC	61	No Nu Ny	65	Pe-f Ph Pi	68	Ra	72	Sc Sh	76	Sta Ste Sti	80	Te Th Ti	84	U	87	We	90	Wr-u-y	94
Mi	56	McD to McK	62	O	66	Pl Po	69	Re Rh Ri	73	Sk Sl	77	Sto-r-u-y	81	To	85			Wh	91	X-Odd	95
Mo	57	McL to McZ	63	Odd	95	Pr to Pz	70	Ro Ru Ry	74	Sm Sn	78	Su-v-w-y-z	82	Tr-u-w-y-z	86	V	88	Wi	92	Y-Z	96

There may be a few names which this Key Table does not classify. All such names are indexed with those beginning X; Sheet No. 95.

No. 96 { This Cott Key Table Index divides Names into 96 Groups according to FIRST TWO LETTERS of SURNAMES (Martin 54), or FIRST TWO LETTERS of First Principal Word of Corporation or Firm Names (The J. C. Brooks Mfg. Company 10 disregarding prefix "The" Groups start on front of numbered sheets and continue on back. Extra sheets in back of book to insert where required which should be numbered alike both sides (preferably red ink) same as original sheet.

Figure 1-7. This Cott index divides names into 96 groups according to first two letters of the surname. (And, the first two letters of the principal name of a corporation.) Thus, the surname of GLASS would be on page 34. The surname of POPE would be on page 69. The JASPER CORPORATION can be found on page 43.

COTTCO UNIVERSAL INDEX

This index (see Figure 1-8) includes columns to "Set Out" common surnames. Those not "Set Out" are in the "Mixed Name Groups" at the bottom of the same index page.

Figure 1-8 above is the top of a page of the Cottco Universal Index. First, look for the surname in the divisions "Set Out" along the top. In this case, RAINEY is shown as page 8. The names that are common in the locality will be listed here, if they fall into the range of letters shown. If REYNOLDS is common in the county, it would also be listed here.

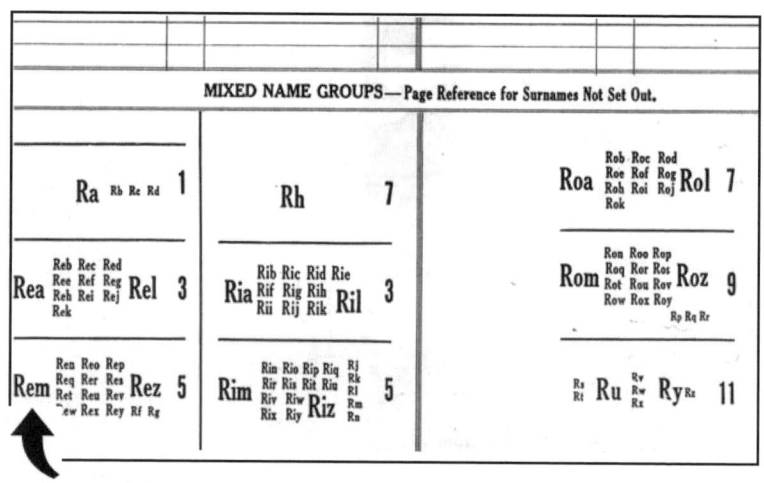

Figure 1-9. If the name does not fall into one of the common surnames that are "Set Out" at the top of the page, it falls into the "Mixed Name Groups" at the bottom of the page. If REMINGTON is not "Set Out" (at the top), check page 5 of the Mixed Name Group.

CHAPTER 1: *The Cott Indexes* 13

THE PAUL CO.

The illustrated index in Figure 1-10 was made by The Cott Index company, but distributed by The Paul Company. First, an index of surnames listed the names and page number. Upon accessing the page number, an "inventory" of the estate appeared. Each of the listed items in the estate included the Book and Page reference for the document. This is similar to the Proceedings Index shown in Chapter 4 except in most cases the index distributed by Paul included both the surname index, and the sub-index with the estate inventory, in the same book.

BNAME INITIAL TAB and sheet for page reference.			Made by The Cott Index Company, Sold by The Paul Company, Baltin
FILE No.	**NAME OF ESTATE**		**DESIGNATION**
1005	GERTRUDE M. TAWNEY		
EXECUTOR, ADM'R, G'D'N OR TRUSTEE			

MONTH	DAY	YEAR	ABSTRACT OF PROCEEDINGS
Aug.	25	1944	First and Final Account
Dec.	18	1944	Discharge

➤ FILE #1005 Gertrude M. Tawney –
FILMED O.C.REEL #12 Pg. #15342

Figure 1-10. First the name of TAWNEY was found in an alphabetical surname index in the front part of this index book which cited the page on which the above illustration was located. Several other entries appeared on the same page in the same format as that shown for Gertrude M. Tawney. The book and page reference to locate the major documents are shown. The first entry is in the Acct. (Account) Book and the 2nd entry is in O.C. (Orphan's Court) Book 1 p. 271. The file number (which contains the loose original papers) is given in the upper left. That number will lead you to that original file, by supplying the clerk with the number shown. In this case, the clerk's office has since microfilmed these records: the added note shows the reel number, and page number of the film.

CHAPTER 2
THE RUSSELL INDEX

The Russell index was a common indexing system (and still is in some states such as Pennsylvania). This search starts with an index book bearing the initial letter of the surname on the spine. Once you have that book in hand, disregard the initial letter of the surname and instead continue for a search within that index book for the first key letter of l, m, n, r, or t.

The index books are arranged alphabetically on shelves. The initial letter of the surname is on the spine, or in some cases, several are in one book. (For example, surnames starting with W, X, Y and Z may all be in the same index book. If so, all those initials "WXYZ" will appear on the spine.) If a surname has extensive listings, there may be two books which cover the entries. W-a and W-n would indicate that the first contains surnames which start with Wa up to Wn, and the W-n book would continue with the rest.

There may be several sets of such indexes, covering various spans of years. Locate the index for the appropriate time period, and for the specific records you seek (If searching land records there may indexes for Grantors, another set for Grantees, etc. For probate records there may be an index to bonds, an index to estate files, etc. Be sure you are in the right indexes.)

THE SEARCH IN FIGURE 2-1

1. Locate the index which shows on the spine the initial letter of the surname you are researching.

2. Assume that you now have the "K" index book in hand, indicating that it includes all surnames starting with K. In this index book within the front few pages (or inside the cover) locate the chart as depicted in Figure 2-1. Since you are already in the "K" book, now disregard the first letter of the surname. Look instead for the first "Key Letter" in the surname, that is, either l, m, n, r, or t. You will seek the *first* key letter *which follows the initial letter of the surname.*

For example, for the surname of KELLY, "e" is not a key letter. The first "key letter" in that name is l. You need to search no further. Using Figure 2-1, find the key letter "l" along the top row. Next you will use the section numbers listed under "l" as shown in the illustration, i.e., 11, 21, 31, 41, 51, and 61.

3. To find a specific person, your next step is to determine which column you will use for the first name. Check the column along the left, titled "Given Name Initials." These represent the initial letter of the first name. Looking for JOHN KELLY? Go to section 31. Looking for WILHEMINA KELLY? She will be in section 51.

> The numbers represent section numbers. Each section will include a number of pages. These usually are represented by numbers as "36-1," "36-2," or "36-a," "36-b," etc.

TO LOCATE NAMES IN INDEX

l-m-n-r-t
Reg. U.S. Pat. Off.

Determine first key-letter following initial letter in Family Name. Find section number in the column headed by said key-letter, opposite given name initial desired. Names not containing a key-letter will be located under "Misc." Corporations, etc., will be located under the first key-letter following the initial letter in the first word of the name, or if no key-letter, under "Misc." Always omit the article "The."

Given Name Initials	Key Letters and Section Numbers					
	l	m	n	r	t	Misc.
ABCD	11	12	13	14	15	16
EFGHI	21	22	23	24	25	26
JKL	31	32	33	34	35	36
MNOPQR	41	42	43	44	45	46
STUVWXYZ	51	52	53	54	55	56
Corps., etc.	61	62	63	64	65	66

RUSSELL INDEX COMPANY, PITTSBURGH, PA.

Figure 2-1. Example of the Russell index based on key letters of l, m, n, r, and t. Each index book will display this chart.

Let's try it again. If looking for all entries for the surname PENTON (still in Figure 2-1), start in the index book with the letter "P" on the spine. Once in that index book, check for the first key letter. The letter "e" (in PENTON) is not a key letter, but the next letter "n" qualifies. For all instances of the surname you'll need to look at pages/sections 13, 23, 33, 43, and 53, and for corporations section 63. Following the method given, to specifically find ARTHUR PENTON go to section 13. For GEORGE PENTON, go to section 23.

SURNAMES WITH NO KEY LETTERS

What about a name with no key letters? If you are looking for the surname ROBB, note that after the initial R of the surname, there are no key letters. Those surnames with no key letters will use the "Misc." column in Figure 2-1. If the specific name is ALAN ROBB, look along the left for given names starting with the grouping of "ABCD" since Alan falls there. Then look across the right to the Misc. column. Any listing for an ALAN ROBB will be section 16.

BREAK-OUTS OF SOME SURNAMES

The figure below shows the break-out of names in the Miscellaneous section, explained on the next page.

Misc		Misc		Misc			
Powe		1 Quick		6 Rowe		6 Read	11
Paye	1			Roe		6 Reid	11
Pope	1			Raub		7 Rhoads	11
Pease	2			Robb		7 Rhodes	11
Page	2			Reeves		7 Reckhow	14
Peck	4			Roush		7 Rezeau	14
Pike	5			Rush		7 Ressemie	14

(Section 36, page 1 — GRANTOR l-m-n-r-t INDEX)

Figure 2-2. This illustrates a break-out of surnames. It is found at the top of the first page of a section, in this case, the Miscellaneous section. If the chart in Figure 2-1 leads you to section 36, look at the first page of that section (note the 1 below 36 shown above indicating it is the first page). Note that various surnames that have been assigned their own page number.

CHAPTER 2: *The Russell Index*

The first page of the Miscellaneous section will have at the top the break-out of some of the names in that section. Usually these are the most common names, but sometimes *all* of the surnames appearing in the Miscellaneous section are assigned their own page in the break-out. In Figure 2-2, note the names. ROBB (which we've already seen falls into the Miscellaneous section) has been assigned 7 so proceed to 36-7 (i.e., section 36 page 7).

The Search in Figures 2-1 and 2-2

1. Using Figure 2-1, look for LOTT ROBB. Note that it would appear in Miscellaneous section 36.

2. Find the initial page (36-1 or 36-a) of section 36 and note that at the top of that page (as shown in Figure 2-2 on the previous page) some surnames have been assigned *their own page within section 36*. To the right of the name Robb is a 7.

3. Now go to page 36-7 (section 36 page 7); there you will find the ROBB surname entries all listed together.

Some areas created an individual page for each surname. Others only did so if that surname had many entries. Any surnames not listed in the break-out should be in the section assigned in Figure 2-1. Check all pages of the section if necessary.

> **The break-out illustrated in Figure 2-2 is most commonly found on the first page of the "Misc." section, but it may be used on the first page of any key letter section so be sure to check. Otherwise important records may be lost.**

Heavily Populated Areas

In some areas where the sheer number of entries is heavy, the Russell index may be further refined (Figure 2-3) by including a second key letter, combined with the first. Each of these are assigned a section number (see this illustrated in Figure 2-2). In this type of amplified Russell system, you need to determine the first and second key letters in the surname, but still starting with the basic key numbers of l, m, n, r, or t.

The Search in Figure 2-3

1. If you are researching the name of ROMINE, go to the index with "R" on the spine.

2. Once there, find the chart at the front of the book and check the left column for MN, the *first and second key letters* in the ROMINE name.

3. To find ALEXANDER ROMINE, look to the top row letters which are shown as "Given Name Initials and Section Numbers." Use the column under A for the given name of Alexander; entries for him will appear on page 120. BERNARD ROMINE would be on page 220.

CHAPTER 2: *The Russell Index*   21

TO LOCATE NAMES IN THE INDEX

Determine the first and second Key-letters after the initial letter in the Surname. In the column headed by the Given Name initial of the name for which you are searching, and opposite the Key-letters contained in the Surname, the number of the section is designated where the name will be found. Duplications of the same Key-letter are disregarded. Surnames, not containing a Key-letter, are found in the sections designated by the numbers opposite "Misc." All names other than those of individuals are found in the sections designated by the numbers in the column headed "Corps., Etc.", and opposite the Key-letters contained in the first word of the name, disregarding the article "The."

LETTERS KEY.	\multicolumn{16}{c}{GIVEN NAME INITIALS AND SECTION NUMBERS}	LETTERS KEY.
	A	B	C	D	E	F	G	HI	J	KL	M	NO	PQ	R	S	TUV	W X Y Z	Corps. Etc.	
L	110	210	310	410	510	610	710	810	910	1010	1110	1210	1310	1410	1510	1610	1710	1810	L
LM	110	210	310	410	510	610	710	810	910	1010	1110	1210	1310	1410	1510	1610	1710	1810	LM
LN	110	210	310	410	510	610	710	810	910	1010	1110	1210	1310	1410	1510	1610	1710	1810	LN
LR	110	210	310	410	510	610	710	810	910	1010	1110	1210	1310	1410	1510	1610	1710	1810	LR
LT	110	210	310	410	510	610	710	810	910	1010	1110	1210	1310	1410	1510	1610	1710	1810	LT
M	120	220	320	420	520	620	720	820	920	1020	1120	1220	1320	1420	1520	1620	1720	1820	M
ML	120	220	320	420	520	620	720	820	920	1020	1120	1220	1320	1420	1520	1620	1720	1820	ML
MN	120	220	320	420	520	620	720	820	920	1020	1120	1220	1320	1420	1520	1620	1720	1820	MN
MR	120	220	320	420	520	620	720	820	920	1020	1120	1220	1320	1420	1520	1620	1720	1820	MR
MT	120	220	320	420	520	620	720	820	920	1020	1120	1220	1320	1420	1520	1620	1720	1820	MT
N	130	230	330	430	530	630	730	830	930	1030	1130	1230	1330	1430	1530	1630	1730	1830	N
NL	130	230	330	430	530	630	730	830	930	1030	1130	1230	1330	1430	1530	1630	1730	1830	NL
NM	130	230	330	430	530	630	730	830	930	1030	1130	1230	1330	1430	1530	1630	1730	1830	NM
NR	130	230	330	430	530	630	730	830	930	1030	1130	1230	1330	1430	1530	1630	1730	1830	NR
NT	130	230	330	430	530	630	730	830	930	1030	1130	1230	1330	1430	1530	1630	1730	1830	NT
R	140	240	340	440	540	640	740	840	940	1040	1140	1240	1340	1440	1540	1640	1740	1840	R
RL	140	240	340	440	540	640	740	840	940	1040	1140	1240	1340	1440	1540	1640	1740	1840	RL
RM	140	240	340	440	540	640	740	840	940	1040	1140	1240	1340	1440	1540	1640	1740	1840	RM
RN	140	240	340	440	540	640	740	840	940	1040	1140	1240	1340	1440	1540	1640	1740	1840	RN
RT	140	240	340	440	540	640	740	840	940	1040	1140	1240	1340	1440	1540	1640	1740	1840	RT
T	150	250	350	450	550	650	750	850	950	1050	1150	1250	1350	1450	1550	1650	1750	1850	T
TL	150	250	350	450	550	650	750	850	950	1050	1150	1250	1350	1450	1550	1650	1750	1850	TL
TM	150	250	350	450	550	650	750	850	950	1050	1150	1250	1350	1450	1550	1650	1750	1850	TM
TN	150	250	350	450	550	650	750	850	950	1050	1150	1250	1350	1450	1550	1650	1750	1850	TN
TR	150	250	350	450	550	650	750	850	950	1050	1150	1250	1350	1450	1550	1650	1750	1850	TR
Misc.	160	260	360	460	560	660	760	860	960	1060	1160	1260	1360	1460	1560	1660	1760	1860	Misc.
	A	B	C	D	E	F	G	HI	J	KL	M	NO	PQ	R	S	TUV	W X Y Z	Corps. Etc.	

Figure 2-3. This variation of the Russell index breaks the key letters of l, m, n, r, and t even further in more populated areas. Note that in this variation the key letters are displayed along the left and right, and the given name initial is along the top. Compare to Figure 2-1.

CHAPTER 3
GRAVES TABULAR INITIAL INDEX

This index, known as Graves' Index, is popular in New York and some other areas. It leads the researcher to the surname index entries by the use of the first three letters of the surname.

In Figure 3-1, the large initial at the top left of the chart is the first letter of the surname.

The second letter of the surname is beneath the initial letter, along the left. The third letter of the surname is at the top, left to right.

THE SEARCH IN FIGURE 3-1

1. Start by finding the index book with the initial letter of the surname. If we seek ABRAMS we'll look for the "A" index book. With that book in hand, note that inside the cover or on the first page or two of that index book is a chart with the initial letter of "A" in large type at the left, confirming you are in the right index.

2. Now you need to find the second letter of the surname, in this case, B. That is along the left in a vertical listing, with A B C combined.

DIVISION TABLES TO GRAVES' TABULAR INITIAL INDEXES.

Entered according to Act of Congress, in the year 1866, by W. H. Graves, in the Clerk's Office of the District Court of the United States for the Northern District of N. Y.

A	A	B	C	D	E	F	G	H	I	J	K	L	M	N	O	P	Q	R	S	T	U	V	W	X	Y	Z
ABC	1	4	6	7	10	13	13	14	14	14	15	16	19	21	22	22	22	23	24	25	26	26	26	26	26	26
D	2	"	"	"	"	"	"	"	"	"	"	"	"	"	"	"	"	"	"	"	"	"	"	"	"	"
EFG	4	"	"	"	"	"	"	"	"	"	"	"	"	"	"	"	"	"	"	"	"	"	"	"	"	"
HIK	"	"	"	"	"	"	"	"	"	"	"	"	"	"	"	"	"	"	"	"	"	"	"	"	"	"
L	"	5	"	"	11	"	"	"	"	"	"	17	"	"	"	"	"	"	"	"	"	"	"	"	"	"
M	"	"	"	"	12	"	"	"	"	"	"	19	"	"	"	"	"	"	"	"	"	"	"	"	"	"
N	"	"	"	8	"	"	"	"	"	"	"	"	"	"	"	"	"	"	"	"	"	"	"	"	"	"
P	"	"	"	10	"	"	"	"	"	"	"	"	"	"	"	"	"	"	"	"	"	"	"	"	"	"
RS	"	"	"	"	"	"	"	"	"	"	"	"	20	"	"	"	"	"	"	"	"	"	"	"	"	"
TUV	"	"	"	"	"	"	"	"	"	"	16	"	"	"	"	"	"	"	"	"	"	"	"	"	"	"
WXYZ	"	"	"	"	"	"	"	"	"	"	"	"	"	"	"	"	"	"	"	"	"	"	"	"	"	"

Figure 3-1. As can be seen above, this is the index book for surnames starting with A. Find the second letter of the surname in the left hand column, and the third letter in the horizontal alphabetical listing. ANDERSON would be on page 8. APPLETON would be on page 22. (Given names are not considered in the Graves Index.)

3. Now look for the third letter in ABRAMS, an R, along the top left to right. ABRAMS would be on page 23.

The surname of ATCHESON would be on page 6.

There is no division by the first name in the Graves Index; it is indexed strictly by the first three letters of the surname.

Note that ditto marks are used rather than to repeat the same page number.

Though the Graves Index is a simple system, it can be confusing as sometimes users misinterpret the left column as referring to the initial letter of the surname.

Distributed also by Lusk, it was sometimes referred to as the Lusk Index.

Chapter 4
PROCEEDINGS INDEX

Proceedings Indexes are used in a few states, for example, Pennsylvania, Delaware, New Jersey, and Maryland. It involves the use of two books—the estate index, and the "Proceedings" index (sometimes called Proceedings Docket).

ESTATE INDEX

The first part of this system (Figures 4-1 and 4-2) is an Estate Index with the initial letter of the surname on the spine. If searching ADAMS, go to the index marked with an A; if searching YOUNG, go to the index book which includes Y (in the illustrated case, XY and Z).

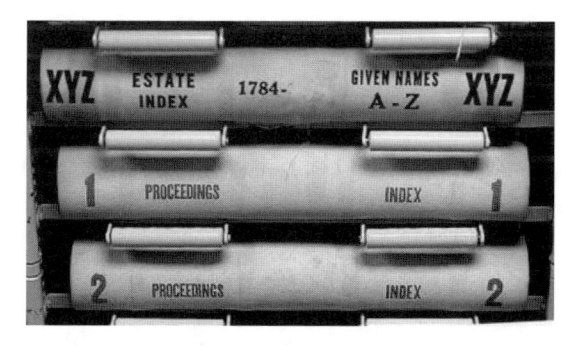

Figure 4-1. At the top is a typical Estate Index. The large XYZ at the left and right represents the initial letter of the surname. "Given Names A-Z" represent the first letter of the first name. Once the name is found in this Estate Index, the researcher proceeds to the book marked "Proceedings Index" shown in Figure 4-3.

File No.	ESTATE		DATE OF DEATH RESIDENCE	PERSONAL REPRESENTATIVE	PROCEEDINGS INDEX		
					Vol.	Page	Blk.
1518	Biggs	George W	Bburg Tp	Thos G Hall-Saml Corle Exrs	1	201	1
1517	Biggs	Garret	Bedmin Tp	John Biggs-A V P Sutphen Exrs	1	200	10
1540	Boice	George		John Boice-John Creed Admrs	1	203	8
1519	Biggs	Hannah (S)	Bburg Tp May 1 1864	Abraham Biggs-Wm P Johnson Exrs	1	201	2
1529	Bush	Gertura Garrett	Bwater Tp Mar 23 1900	Alfred Camman Exr	1	202	5
1516	Biggs	Garret (or) Henrietta	Bedmin Tp Feb 15 1917	John A Biggs Admr-David M Todd Admr dbn	1	200	8

Figure 4-2. The above is the Estate Index, the first part of a two-part system Proceedings index system. First, find the surname and item in the index book with the initial letter of the surname on the spine. Note that it will give you the Volume, Page, and Block numbers. (Note also that the File Number for the original estate files appears at the left. Use this for inquiring to the clerk for the original loose papers.)

THE SEARCH IN FIGURE 4-2

1. If you are looking for GEORGE BIGGS, once you have the Estate Index book in hand which displays the initial letter of the surname on the spine, find him listed.

2. Copy the information for George Biggs, and in particular, be sure to copy the *book, page and block number*.

3. Note that the first George Biggs listing in Figure 4-2 shows George Biggs to be in Volume 1 page 201.

4. Now look around the shelves for the indexes marked PROCEEDINGS (as shown in Figure 4-1).

Turning to page 201 in the same book you would find it divided into "blocks" and a Block number with each. The illustration of the George Biggs block was unavailable for inclusion in this present book but Figure 4-3 shows a similar block in a different estate.

CHAPTER 4 *The Proceedings Index* 27

Though the illustration in Figure 4-3 is for a GEORGE ALBERT and not for Biggs referred to Figure 4-2, it will illustrate what is found in a "block." The block will be titled with the name of the estate, the name of the person who handled the estate (normally executor, administrator, or guardian's name), and place of the deceased's or ward's last residence or where death occurred. In a guardianship, the place the minor or ward resides is shown.

7 Albert George	File No. 114			Res. and Date of Death Mar 25 1913 Warren Tp		
PROCEEDING	Dkt.	Vol.	Page	Month	Day	Year
Emma L Albert Admrx						
App for Adm	Ap	11	358	Apr	4	1913
Adm Bd	AB	F	4	Apr	4	1913
Letters of Adm	AG	E	559	Apr	4	1913
Inventory	In	T	390	Apr	22	1913
Rept & Disch	RD	P	248	Jul	7	1913
Rept & Disch	RD	P	249	Jul	7	1913

Figure 4-3 The above is one of the "blocks" in a Proceedings Index (sometimes called a Docket). It inventories the major papers in an estate file, and directs the user to the volume and page where the transcribed documents can be located. In the example, the file number shown should enable you to access the original estate papers. The block entry further provides the filing date of the inventory, and references and filing date for the will and letters testamentary. (The originals of the will, letters, and inventory, should be in the original file; transcribed copies in the given references.) Further, the entry discloses that Emma L. Albert was the administratrix. The column showing "Ap," "AB," etc. are the kind of volumes, in this case, Appearance Docket 11, Administrator's Bond Volume F, etc.

The block may also show the death date (especially in indexes filed in the late 1800s or later). The person appointed to handle the estate (executor, administrator, guardian, etc.) is included.

A listing of the major papers filed in the estate is included with the volume and page where each can be found. The date filed is normally added. Use this information to find each of the cited record books on the shelves.

CHAPTER 5
THE CAMPBELL INDEX

The Campbell Index and other "first name" indexes are not alphabetical by the surname, but by the first or given name. This can help you find your ancestor's listing immediately if you are only looking for a specific person. But if you are checking all listings for the surname (which is often the best strategy), it can be cumbersome.

Find the index with the initial letter of the surname on the spine of the index book. *All* the surnames starting with that letter are listed in it, with no effort to list them alphabetically. They are instead divided by the first name.

Now that you have that index book with the initial letter of the surname in hand, open it and you will find that the entries are alphabetized by the first name. And, even those first names are not in strict alphabetical order.

THE SEARCH IN FIGURE 5-1
1. If you are looking for ALLAN JOHNSON, find the index book with "J" on the spine.

2. Go to the page with the "A" *given* names. ALLAN JOHNSON will be intermingled with others whose surnames start with J, and whose first names start with A, such as Andrew Jackson, Arthur Jamison, etc. If you are

looking for THOMAS JOHNSON, look for the section of "T" given names.

DIVISION OF GIVEN NAMES
Usually 2-4 initial letters are combined for the given names. Perhaps all the A, B, C, and D first names, then E, F, etc.

KNOW NICKNAMES
It is essential to know nicknames when using a first-name index. If you don't know that "Gus" is a nickname for

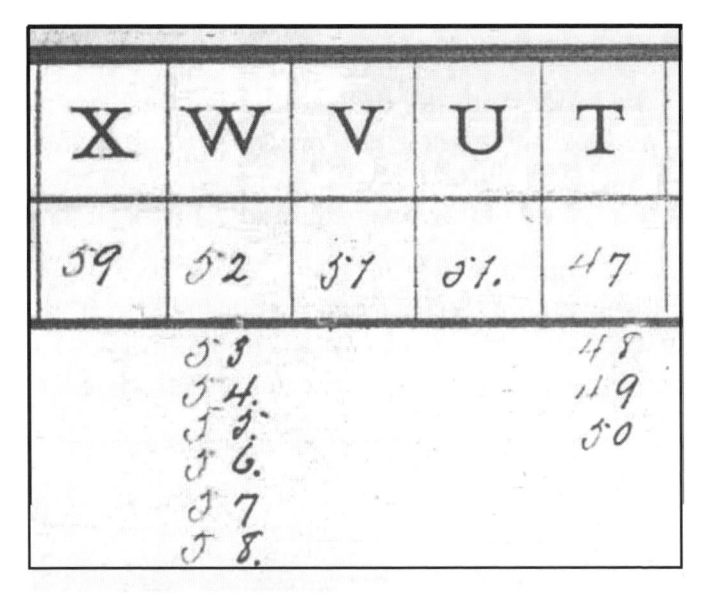

X	W	V	U	T
59	52	57	57	47
	53			48
	54			49
	55			50
	56			
	57			
	58			

Figure 5-1. The above is a typical Campbell index. The letters represent the first name. Entries for given names starting with W would appear on pages 52, 53, 54, 55, 56, 57 and 58. The surname is represented by the initial letter of the surname on the spine of this index book. The above chart will appear on the first one or two pages of the index book, and the entries themselves will be in the same book, on the pages listed.

Augustus, and are looking only under the given names starting with A, you will miss him as "Gus" in the "G" section!

STRATEGIES

It quickly becomes apparent that this is a slow system when searching all entries for a surname. You can't even have the section with the surname photocopied, for the entries will be scattered among many pages throughout the index book. It should be noted, however, that the entries are chronological. Therefore, you can limit the search to the years pertinent to your particular problem in each of the given sections. Check the "A" given name section for entries that start and end with the time period you are searching. When you are finished with that, move on to the "B" section and do the same. That will help speed your effort to find all of the surname entries.

USING SOME SHORTCUTS

1. If you are looking for JOSEPH MARTIN, go to the index book with "M" on the spine.

2. Find the section with the "J" given names.

3. To shorten the search, determine the time period you are searching and, using the column that shows the recordation date, look for Joseph by starting and ending in the time period you are seeking.

4. When you find the entries, take down the Volume and page in which the entries appear, and then proceed to find those volumes of records on the shelves.

CHAPTER 6
THE VOWEL INDEXES

In indexes based on vowels, the surnames are by the initial letter of the surname and the first vowel that comes after the initial letter. For example, a surname starting with "T" would have the following subdivisions: "TA," "TE," "TI," "TO," "TU," and "TY." In "TA" it would bring together surnames of Tarleton, Tarry, Tanner, and Tathill.

THE VARIATIONS
There are several variations on how these are displayed, or even combined with other styles of indexes. One variation is used with an "item" system. It consists of two indexes and is illustrated in Figures 6-1 and 6-2. (The illustrations are for a Grantor index but this can be used for other types of documents as well.)

THE SEARCH IN FIGURE 6-1
1. The researcher looking for deeds of ADAM ROSS would start with the Grantor index including R surnames for the proper time period.

2. There are usually some type of tab or index divisions. Figure 6-1 shows a tabbed index. To find ADAM ROSS find the R tab. (The illustration shows tabs only down to the letter H but the actual index did go to R.)

3. Opening the index at the R tab, it is divided by vowels following the initial letter of R. In this case, turn to the page which shows a division for o, u, or y (see Figure 6-1). There, ADAM ROSS is listed, and by his name an Item Number 264 is listed on page 19. Note both of these numbers.

4. Next, turning to page 19 of the same index (see Figure 6-2) it will be noted that the ADAM ROSS entries are at the bottom of the illustration which include all the grantor entries for him.

Looking specifically for Item 264 which we had seen referenced in Figure 6-1, we now find in Figure 6-2 that item. It shows that Adam Ross granted to Chas. Gallagher on July 4, 1767, land in Chambersburg, recorded in Book 1 p. 433. With the latter reference, you can now find Book 1 p. 433 for the full document.

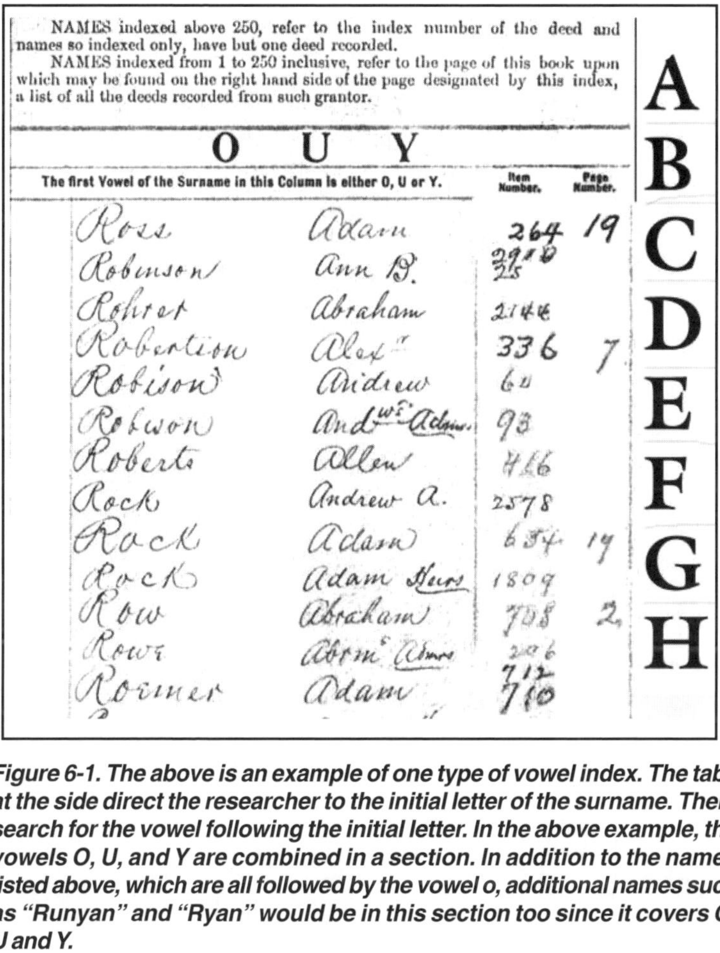
NAMES indexed above 250, refer to the index number of the deed and names so indexed only, have but one deed recorded.
NAMES indexed from 1 to 250 inclusive, refer to the page of this book upon which may be found on the right hand side of the page designated by this index, a list of all the deeds recorded from such grantor.

O U Y

The first Vowel of the Surname in this Column is either O, U or Y.		Item Number.	Page Number.
Ross	Adam	264	19
Robinson	Ann B.	29 / 25	
Rohrer	Abraham	2144	
Robertson	Alexr	336	7
Robison	Andrew	60	
Robison	Andw Adm.	93	
Roberts	Allen	466	
Rock	Andrew A.	2578	
Rock	Adam	654	19
Rock	Adam Heirs	1809	
Row	Abraham	708	2
Rowe	Abrm Adms	206	
Romer	Adam	712 / 710	

Figure 6-1. The above is an example of one type of vowel index. The tabs at the side direct the researcher to the initial letter of the surname. Then, search for the vowel following the initial letter. In the above example, the vowels O, U, and Y are combined in a section. In addition to the names listed above, which are all followed by the vowel o, additional names such as "Runyan" and "Ryan" would be in this section too since it covers O, U and Y.

COURTHOUSE INDEXES ILLUSTRATED

William Rea   19

AREA.		Item Number.	GRANTEES.	Date of Record.			Place of Record.		LOCATION.
Acres.	Perches.			Month.	Day.	Year.	Book.	Page.	
One	74	417	Thos. Kirby	Dec.	10	1805	7	68	Chambersburg
		781	Wm. Mentzer	Nov.	24	1820	15	219	Greene
		788	Jno. S. Kerr.	May	18	1831	15	354	"
166	66								
186	60								
186 and Lots	1/7 19.94.90								

Adam Ross

		264	Chas. Gallagher	July	4	1787	1	433	Chambersburg
		760	Joseph Ross	May	7	1829	14	580	Guilford
		857	Saml. Dunn	Dec	2	1835	17	23	Path Valley
	121	269	John Penn Jr. &al	June	10	1787	2	81	Lurgan

Figure 6-2. The above is the second part of an index which first led the researcher to a listing of the name and a page number, plus a specific item number (see Figure 6-1). Proceeding to the page (19 in this case) the item on Adam Ross was found, bringing together all items in which he was grantor. We were seeking item 264, which is shown above as a deed to Chas. Gallagher. With that reference you can now go to the deed book listed, Bk 1 p. 433, to find the full deed.

Chapter 7
The Stark Index

Stark's System of Indexing is not too widely used, but needs to be understood when it is encountered. The initial letter of the surname is at the top of the chart. The index is a combination of the first and second letters of the surname, and the first letter of the given or Christian name.

The Search in Figure 7-1

1. If you seek FRANK RAFFERTY, go to the surname R (which is represented in the large R in Figure 7-1).

2. Next, look for the *second letter of the surname*, in this case, A. You will find it at the left in the vertical alphabet.

3. Then look for the initial letter of the given name, represented by the horizontal alphabet left to right. Note that F (for Frank) will be on page 395.

4. Go to page 395. There you would find any listings for FRANK RAFFERTY (as well as others who fall on that page).

If you were looking for URIAH RAFFERTY, he will be on page 588.

STARK'S SYSTEM OF INDEXING.

This Index Key is a combination of the first letter of the Christian Name, and the first and second letters of the Sur-name. The horizontal column represents the first letter of Christian Name. The large letter representing the first letter of Sur-name, and the perpendicular column representing the second letter of the same. Thereby dividing the alphabet (if necessary) into 18,252 combinations.

DIRECTIONS.—Put your finger on the letter of the Christian Name, follow down the column to the second letter of Sur-name where you will find the page for said combination.

Entered according to Act of Congress, in the year 1872, by George Stark, in the office of the Librarian of Congress, at Washington.

R

	A	B	C	D	E	F	G	H	I	John	Jo.	J	K	L	M	N	O	P	Q	R	S	T	U	V	W	X
A	339	350	355	368	376	395	397	414	423	429	444	482	505	506	509	529	534	536	541	541	549	575	588	588	589	606
B																										
C																										
D																										
E	339	360	355	368	376	395	397	414	423	429	444	482	505	506	509	529	534	536	541	541	549	578	588	588	589	606
F																										
G																										

Figure 7-1. The above is Stark's Index. In the illustration, the initial letter of the surname is R. Next, the second letter is represented by the column at the left, top to bottom. Once that has been established, look for the initial letter of the given name in the left to right alphabet column along the top. In the illustrated index above, the name of FRANK RAFFERTY would be on 395.

CHAPTER 8
DEVISOR AND DEVISEE INDEXES

The devisor and devisee index is only available in a few courthouses, but when it is found, it is of tremendous value. It is particularly located in North Carolina, and occasionally in other locations.

If your ancestor was the recipient of a devise (that is, the recipient of real property through a will), the land passed to him or her through probate proceedings. Deeds were generally not required to be recorded in such instances. Many years could pass without any trace in the land recordings if it was not for devisor and devisee indexes. Recognizing that it would be helpful to have an index to track these inheritances, North Carolina handled that problem though these unique indexes.

DEVISOR INDEX. Lists the name of the devisor (the testator who devised land). This index is somewhat redundant; the testator index would also turn up the same will, though you wouldn't know that the will included land from a testator index alone.

DEVISEE INDEX. A devisee was the recipient of a devise of real property through a will. A relationship almost impossible to otherwise determine may surface through a devisee index. If Susan Baldwin inherited a tract from her grandfather Jonathan Walters, and you knew nothing of a Walters connection, how would you know of the

Walters will naming Susan as "granddaughter"? With a devisee index you'd readily find it. You would search the surname of BALDWIN with which you are familiar. Under "B" Susan Baldwin would be listed as a devisee. After her name, the name Jonathan Walters would appear as devisor (testator), with the will reference. This leads you easily to that will naming his granddaughter Susan. Many unsuspected relationships have been disclosed because of these devisee indexes.

Though North Carolina is the only state which routinely used such an index, occasionally it will be found elsewhere in a county courthouse. In other areas it may be under a different name, such as "Heirs by Descent."

Figure 8-1. The above is a devisee index, that is, the person who is a recipient of the devise of real property is indexed at the left. In the first entry the name of the devisee and the devisor (testator) is the same, and would easily have been found by a JONES researcher even in the will book. The second entry likewise would also have been easy to find via a will book. However, in the third entry, showing Senia James as the devisee (recipient of a devise), the researcher who didn't know there was a possible WHITE family connection may now have an important new clue in the cited will of Bridget White. Bridget was likely related (to have devised land to Senia James) which can be confirmed (or not) by examining the full will of Bridget White.

Chapter 9
TRADITIONAL INDEXES

There are many traditional, "straight-forward" indexes in use. These include indexes which are alphabetized by the last name, in alphabetical order of that surname, and perhaps then alphabetized by the given name. Thus, this index might show in the "A" surname section:

Abrams
    Donald, p 9
    Joseph, p 405
    Manuel, p 369
Adams
    Margaret, John, p 20
    Norton, p 185
    Thomas, p 65
Ahern
    Aaron, p 565
    Benjamin, p 483
    Joseph, p 25
Ammons
    John, p 65
    Kenneth, p 85
    Mary and Matilda, p 222
Atkinson
    William, p 342
    Wilson, p 95

When indexes were prepared for individual record books, they are simply alphabetized by initial letter of the surname. There aren't usually that many of each to create a problem. Thus, the clerk created a surname section A, B, C, D, etc. Every document that was recorded in that book was generally entered by the initial letter of their surname, chronologically. Thus you might see an index such as that in Figure 9-1. It was later, when indexes were consolidated to cover a larger span of years, that the large variety of indexes came into use.

CHAPTER 9: Traditional Indexes

V		W	
Vanderwolf Cornelius. Account	24	Ward Thomas Account	12
Venables Benjamin Account	85	Whayland Thomas Account	22
Ditto Addl. Ditto	113	ditto distribution	23
Ditto Finl ditto & Dis	117	Williams Levin Account	34
Venables Robert Finl Ditto	124	Walston Henry Account	35
Venables Rebecca Finl Acct & Dis	183	Walston Jno. Distribution	38
Vennables Joseph Finl acct	221	Waller Willm Acct to Rich Waller	47
The Same Distribution	322	Guardian	
		Whitney Thomas Acct & distrib	52
		Walston Henry f acct & distribu	56
		Whitney Sarah & others rect to	
		wmy Joseph Whitney Executors of	
		Thomas Whitney	57
		Williams Thomas Account	77
		Walston Henry Acct & distrib	84
P. continued		Witkins Saml decd receipts by	
Porter Joshua 2d Acct	225	John Witkins Mary Ann Witkins	6
Porter William acct & distrib	226	Sally Witkins John H Adams	
Pollitt James acct & distrib.	231	Witkins & Samuel Witkins	
Porter &c & others receipts	243	Woolford Thomas D. Account	94
Porter William T. Acct & Distri	263	Wilson James Account	106
Porter Joshua Account	289	Walter Thomas Ditto	108
		Waters Richard Account	123
		Ditto Finl D Distrib	126
		White Thomas Account	139
		Ditto Addl Acct & Distribution	142
		Whillingham Hibur Acct	151

Figure 9-1. This is a simple index, by initial letter of the surname, and items entered as filed or recorded. Note that "P" was continued to the "V" page in this index when the "P" section was full. A notation also appeared at the bottom of the "P" page advising of the continuance.

MINUTE BOOKS

The minute books may or may not contain an index. If they do, it likely will be a traditional index (such as illustrated in Figure 9-1), except that each entry will show the subject of the entry, and perhaps a brief note such as "bond of," or "continuance."

COURT ORDER BOOK (COB)

Since the counties generally required by law that the court's orders be recorded, Court Order Books should have an index. However, whether the index has survived time may be a factor.

The indexes for court orders may be an index only to the plaintiff (in matters when there is a plaintiff and defendant), or it may also index the defendant. When indexing the plaintiff, the action will show an entry such as:

  Bostian, Samuel vs Holmes, George, debt, p. 85

If the COB also indexes defendants, the same action would be shown again under H as:

  Holmes, George, ads Samuel Bostian, debt, p. 85

"Ads" in this case is "Ad sectam" which means "at the suit of." It is the opposite of "versus."

CHAPTER 10
AND OTHERS ...

There are a variety of indexes that do not fall into the chapters thus far presented. They will be discussed and illustrated here.

COMMON VARIATIONS

Figure 10-1 is an index by three letters of the surname, then by first initial of the given name. For another variation, this one by Hall & McChesney, see Figure 10-2.

THE SEARCH IN FIGURE 10-2

1. Looking for ELI CARROLL? Find the index book which includes "C." In the example, the index book includes surnames starting with A, B, and C. Note that the "C" section shows a large C at the top of the column, so you know you are now in surnames starting with a C.

2. Now look for the second letter of the surname, along the vertical column on the left. For CARROLL, the second letter is an A. Note that there are two columns showing "A." One shows "A-M" and the other shows "N-Z" which are divisions for the next step.

3. The third letter of CARROLL is an R, so pick the column which shows A (for second letter) and N-Z (for third letter). This shows page 47, which you'll examine to find the entries.

COURTHOUSE INDEXES ILLUSTRATED

DIVISIONS OF SURNAMES, OR First Part of Corporate Names.	SUBDIVISIONS BY FIRST LETTER OF GIVEN NAME, or First Letter of Second Capitalized part of Firm or Corporate Name containing no Given Name.																					
R	A	B	C	D	E	F	G	H	I	J	K	L	M	N P	O Q	R T	S U	V X	W Y	Z
	Page Sec	Page Sec	Page Sec	Page Sec	Page Sec	Page Sec	Page Sec	Page Sec	Page Sec	Page Sec	Page Sec	Page Sec	Page Sec	Page Sec	Page Sec	Page Sec	Page Sec	Page Sec	Page Sec	Page Sec
Roe Rof Rog	828	828	828	828	828	828	828	828	829	829	829	829	829	829	829	829	829	828		
Roh Roi Roj Rok Rol	830	830	830	830	830	830	830	830	830	830	830	830	830	830	830	830	830	830		
Rom Ron Roo	831	831	831	831	831	831	831	831	832	832	832	832	832	832	832	832	832	832		
Rop Roq Ror	831	831	831	831	831	831	831	831	832	832	832	832	832	832	832	832	832	832		
Ros Rot Rou	833	833	833	834	834	834	834	835	836	836	836	836	836	837	837	837					
Rov Row Rox Roy Roz	838	838	838	838	838	838	838	838	838	838	838	838	838	838	838	838					
Ru	839	839	840	840	840	840	841	842	842	842	843	843									
Ry Rz	844	844	844	844	844	845	845	845	846	846	846	846	846									

Figure 10-1. A variation of an index by three letters of the surname, and then by the initial letter of the given name. This is in the "R" surname index book. For the surname of ROLAND see the second line on the left for "Roh Roi Roj Rok Rol." For ANDERSON ROLAND see page 830; for Jonathan ROLAND see page 830. For QUINCY ROLAND, go to page 830.

CHAPTER 10: *And Others*

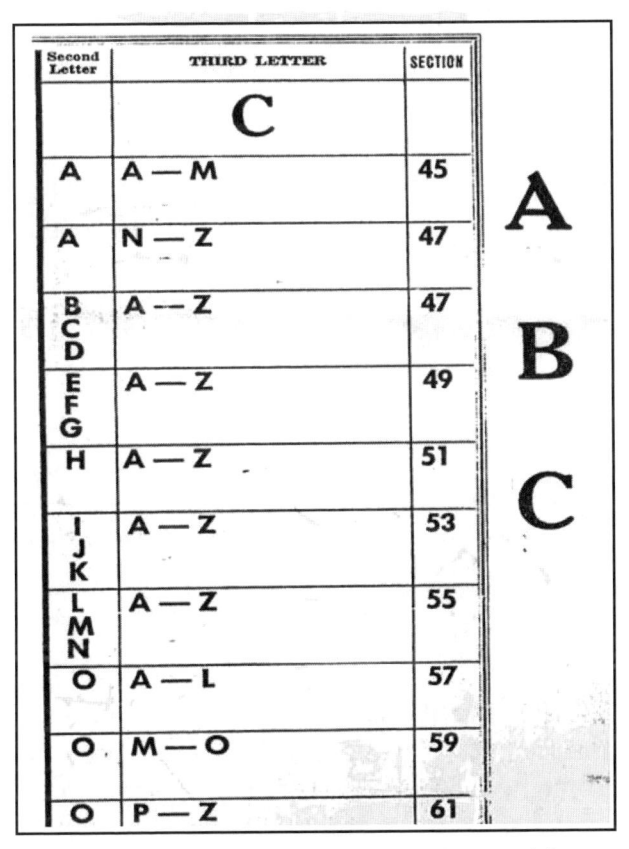

Second Letter	THIRD LETTER	SECTION
	C	
A	A — M	45
A	N — Z	47
B C D	A — Z	47
E F G	A — Z	49
H	A — Z	51
I J K	A — Z	53
L M N	A — Z	55
O	A — L	57
O	M — O	59
O	P — Z	61

Figure 10-2. This variation using the first three letters of the surname is by Hall & McChesney. The tabs along the right side lead the user to surnames starting with A, B, and C. The above shows the section which includes the surnames starting with C. For the surname of CAHILL, see the vertical column along the left for "a" and then for the "h" go to the second column (horizontal) which in this case shows "A-M" on page 45. If looking for JORDAN COTTRELL note that it would be on page 61.

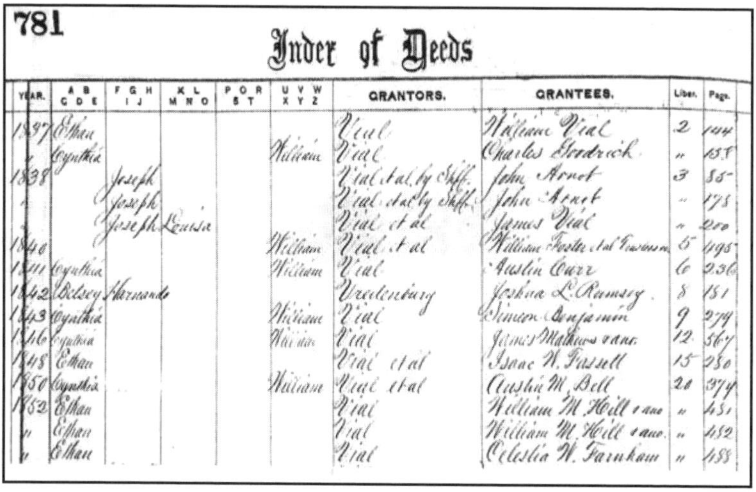

781

Index of Deeds

YEAR.	A B C D E	F G H I J	K L M N O	P Q R S T	U V W X Y Z	GRANTORS.	GRANTEES.	Liber.	Page.
1837	Ethan					Vial	William Vial	2	144
	Cynthia				William	Vial	Charles Goodrich	"	155
1838		Joseph				Vial et al by Shff.	John Arnot	3	55
		Joseph				Vial et al by Shff.	John Arnot	"	175
		Joseph	Louisa			Vial et al	James Vial	"	200
1840					William	Vial et al	William Foster et al Trustees	5	495
1841	Cynthia				William	Vial	Austin Carr	6	236
1842	Betsey	Hernando				Vredenburg	Joshua L. Ramsey	8	181
1843	Cynthia				William	Vial	Simeon Benjamin	9	274
1846	Cynthia				William	Vial	James Mathews et al	12	567
1848	Ethan					Vial et al	Isaac W. Russell	15	280
1850	Cynthia				William	Vial et al	Austin M. Bell	20	374
1852	Ethan					Vial	William M. Hill et al	"	451
"	Ethan					Vial	William M. Hill et al	"	452
"	Ethan					Vial	Celestia W. Farnham	"	453

Figure 10-3. This index, commonly used, is alphabetical by the name of the subject of the entry (in this case, the grantor). Once you find the surname, look next for the columns which divide the given names.

The above variation is a Grantor Index. The surname is shown under the "Grantor" heading. To the left is the year, and then the given name is entered into a column which matches the first letter of the given name. The Grantee is listed to the right, followed by the Record Book Volume and Page number. The entries themselves are entered chronologically in each surname section. That is, under names starting with "V," the entries would be entered by the date of recording of all surnames starting with that letter.

CHAPTER 10: *And Others*

BOLLMAN'S INDEX

This index referred to as Bollman's Index is illustrated in Figure 10-4 and is a simple system. The first letter of the surname runs top to bottom on the left. The first letter of the given name runs left to right along the top.

THE SEARCH IN FIGURE 10-4

1. For the surname of DONALI find D along the left.

2. To find FRANCISCO DONALI use the "F" column to the right of the D column, where given names starting with F will be listed. In this case, page 130 will hold the indexed entry. Perusing that page will supply the details leading the user to the Volume and page containing the full document.

COURTHOUSE INDEXES ILLUSTRATED

BOLLMAN'S INDEX CHART

Directions for Using: The letters at the left of the Chart running from top to bottom represent the first letter of Surname. The letters running from left to right from each Surname Letter, represent the first letter of Christian name. The figure under each letter of Christian name represent the page number of the Index Book upon which the name is found.

	A	B	C	D	E	F	G	H	I	J	K	L	M	N	O	P	Q	R	S	T	U	V	W	X	Y	Z
A	1	1	4	5	6	6	7	8	8	10	15	15	15	15	15	16	17	18	18	20	20	20	21	81	91	91
B	26	27	30	33	35	36	36	40	42	43	53	53	55	58	58	59	61	61	64	68	70	70	70	70	70	70
	A	B	C	D	E	F	G	H	I	J	K	L	M	N	O	P	Q	R	S	T	U	V	W	X	Y	Z
C	75	77	78	80	82	84	86	89	91	92	102	102	104	107	107	109	111	112	114	114	114	116	116	116	116	116
	A	B	C	D	E	F	G	H	I	J	K	L	M	N	O	P	Q	R	S	T	U	V	W	X	Y	Z
D	121	123	124	126	128	130	131	133	135	136	144	144	146	150	150	151	151	153	153	155	155	155	157	157	157	157

Figure 10-4. In Bollman's index the letters at the left on the chart running top to bottom represent the first letter of the surname. The letters running from left to right represent the first letter of the given or Christian name. The figures under each letter of the Christian name represent the page number of the Index Book upon which the name is found. Thus, GEORGE BANNER would be on 36 and Benjamin Dancer would be on page 123.

AN ORPHAN'S COURT INDEX

A few states have Orphan's Courts, including Pennsylvania, Delaware, Maryland, New Jersey, and Alabama. They contain extremely important records involving estates, such as divisions and controversies.

The index to Orphan's Court varies depending upon the system used in the county. Pictured in Figure 10-5 is an index of some guardianship matters showing a chart along the top of the page dividing the surname by one or two letters. Underneath that division are initial letters of the given name. MARIA MUSELLI would be on page 48.

The index illustration gives the subject's name (in this case the ward who is in need of a guardian), the year and volume/page of the appointment of the guardian, the volume and page of the bond, and the listing for any statement or allowance.

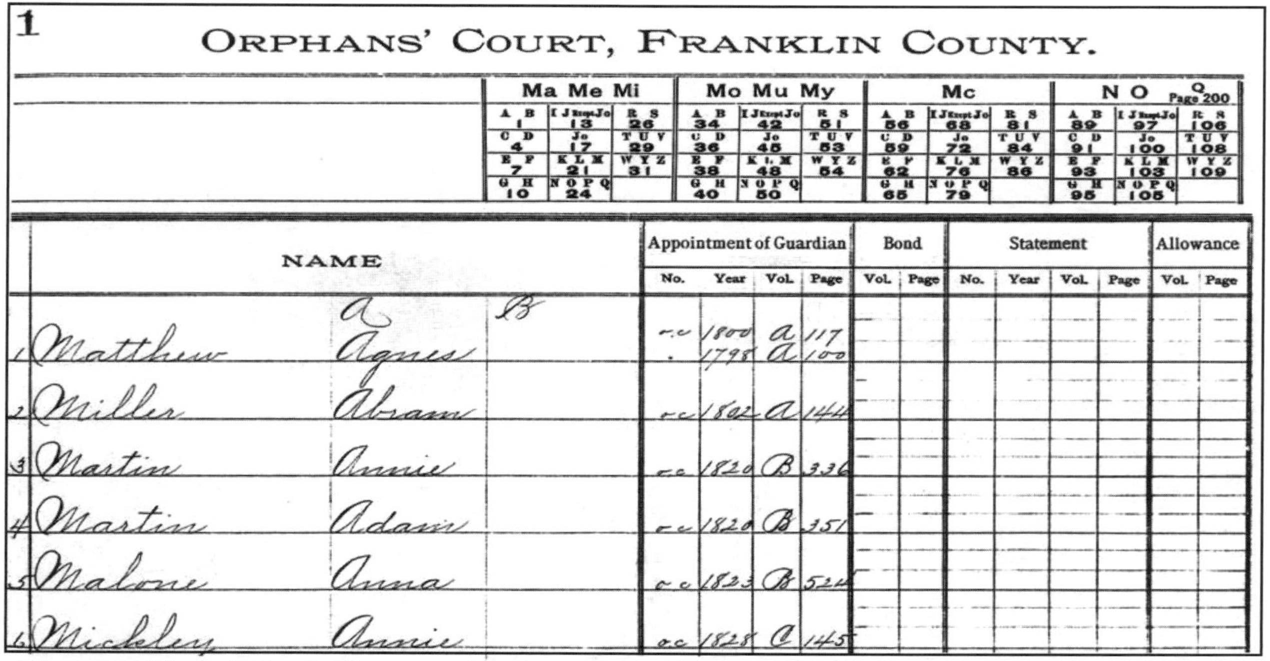

1

ORPHANS' COURT, FRANKLIN COUNTY.

Ma Me Mi			Mo Mu My			Mc			N O		Q Page 200
A B 1	I J Except Jo 13	R S 26	A B 34	I J Except Jo 42	R S 51	A B 56	I J Except Jo 68	R S 81	A B 89	I J Except Jo 97	R S 106
C D 4	Jo 17	T U V 29	C D 36	Jo 45	T U V 53	C D 59	Jo 72	T U V 84	C D 91	Jo 100	T U V 108
E F 7	K L M 21	W Y Z 31	E F 38	K L M 48	W Y Z 54	E F 62	K L M 76	W Y Z 86	E F 93	K L M 103	W Y Z 109
G H 10	N O P Q 24		G H 40	N O P Q 50		G H 65	N O P Q 79		G H 95	N O P Q 105	

	NAME		Appointment of Guardian				Bond		Statement				Allowance	
			No.	Year	Vol.	Page	Vol.	Page	No.	Year	Vol.	Page	Vol.	Page
		A	B											
1	Matthew	Agnes	o.c	1800	A	117								
			.	1798	A	100								
2	Miller	Abram	o.c	1802	A	144								
3	Martin	Annie	o.c	1820	B	336								
4	Martin	Adam	o.c	1820	B	351								
5	Malone	Anna	o.c	1823	B	524								
6	Mickley	Annie	o.c	1828	C	145								

Figure 10-5. An index by the first one or two letters of the surname. Mackley, Meckley and Mickley would be grouped together. Likewise, all those surnames starting with N or O would be grouped together (see the far right column). The illustration is a guardian's index.

CHAPTER 10: *And Others* 53

TOWN HALL INDEXES

In states where the records are kept in Town Halls instead of county courthouses (such as Connecticut), the indexes have often been retyped and are standard alphabetical indexes such as shown for Town meetings in Figure 10-6 below. Records such as deeds are often in typed card indexes in these Town Halls, as are Vital Records. (Connecticut also has Probate Districts encompassing several towns, with indexes similar to those in Town Halls.)

```
Town Hall, vote of thanks to Nelson Hotchkiss for offer, 55.
"      "    Committtee appointed to estimate cost of repairs, 20.
"      "    Selectmen instructed to keep closed, 20.
"      "    Building Committee instructed to procure Steam Heating
            Apparatus, 274; Reconsidered, 275.
"      "    appropriation for Steam Heating, 274; Reconsidered, 275.
"      "    to be rented to outsiders from $10 to $12 and to home
            Societies for $5, 305.
"      "    Parmelee Post to have use of Memorial Day, 319.
"   House, voted to repair, Selectmen a Committee, 27.
```

Figure 10-6. An index for Town Hall meetings in Connecticut.

FIRST NAME VARIATION

In Figure 10-7, the initial letter of the surname is horizontal along the top. Beneath each is a chart of divisions of first names, each with the page number. The illustration is for an index which indexes both grantors and grantees.

THE SEARCH IN FIGURE 10-7

1. Looking for GEORGE ROSE, first go to the "R" along the top column, left to right.

2. Then look for George and note it is page 395.

3. Turn to page 395 and locate the listings.

54   COURTHOUSE INDEXES ILLUSTRATED

					BELMONT COUNTY, OHIO							395	
	H	Mc	N	O	P	Q	R	S	T	U	V	W	X
	M283 A 295 M309		A 319 M333	A 341 M349	A 355 M371	383	A 385 M403	A 415 M437	A 451 M465	475	A 477 M478	A 479 M497	509
	N 285 B 297 N 311		B 321 N 335	B 342 N 350	B 357 N 373		B 387 N 405	B 417 N 439	B 452 N 467		B 477 N 478	B 481 N 499	
	O 285 C 297 O 312		C 321 O 335	C 342 O 350	C 359 O 374		C 389 O 406	C 418 O 440	C 453 O 467		C 477 O 478	C 481 O 499	Y
	286 D299 312		D323 336	D343 350	D361 374		D390 406	D419 441	D455 468		D478 478	D463 500	
	R 287 E 299 R 313		E 323 R 336	E 344 R 351	E 361 R 375		E 391 R 407	E 421 R 443	E 455 R 468		E 478 R 478	E 483 R 501	511
	S 289 F 301 S 314		F 325 S 337	F 345 S 352	F 363 S 377		F 393 S 409	F 423 S 445	F 457 S 469		F 478 S 478	F 485 S 503	
	T 291 G 302 T 315		G 326 T 338	G 345 T 353	G 365 T 379		G 395 T 411	G 425 T 447	G 458 T 471		G 478 T 478	G 486 T 505	Z
	U 292 H 303 U 316		H 327 U 338	H 346 U 353	H 365 U 380		H 397 U 412	H 427 U 448	H 459 U 471		H 478 U 478	H 487 U 506	
	V 292 I 304 V 316		I 328 V 338	I 346 V 353	I 367 V 380		I 398 V 412	I 429 V 448	I 460 V 471		I 478 V 478	I 489 V 506	513
	W293 J 305 W317		J 329 W339	J 347 W354	J 367 W381		J 399 W413	J 431 W419	J 461 W473		J 478 W478	J 491 W507	
	Y 294 K 307 Y 318		K 330 Y 339	K 348 Y 354	K 369 Y 382		K 401 Y 414	K 433 Y 450	K 463 Y 473		K 478 Y 478	K 493 Y 508	
	Z 294 L 308 Z 318		L 331 Z 339	L 348 Z 354	L 369 Z 382		L 401 Z 414	L 435 Z 450	L 463 Z 473		L 478 Z 478	L 495 Z 508	

Date of Deed	NAME	NAME	Vol.	Page	Acres	Sec.	Twp.	Range	Lot	Dollars	Remarks
Mch 30-1832	Rose	Peter	T	O	21	St Clairsville			10-11	450	✓
Sept 5-1832	Rose	Mary B.	T	O	338	St Clairsville			10-11	1	
Jan 5-1836	Ring	Georinga Herfhish	T	to	286	80+19	5	4		300	
May 9-1836	Rose	Dorothea et al	T	to	419	St Clairsville			15-11	66	
Mar 30-1836	Rose	Admr	to	McAlister Jnr	24	53	140 22	9	6	under 45 act	288

Figure 10-7. The initial letter of the surname is left to right at the top. Below each initial letter are divisions by the first name, and the page number. Note that this index is for both grantors and grantees, thus, if George Rose was either a grantor or a grantee his entries would be on page 395. How do we know that? Note the column showing "F" or "to" for this indicates that the person named in the left hand column is either being granted the land FROM the person on the right, or is granting the land TO the person on the right. If this "to" of "F" column is overlooked, it can cause considerable confusion in understanding and reconstructing the family's records.

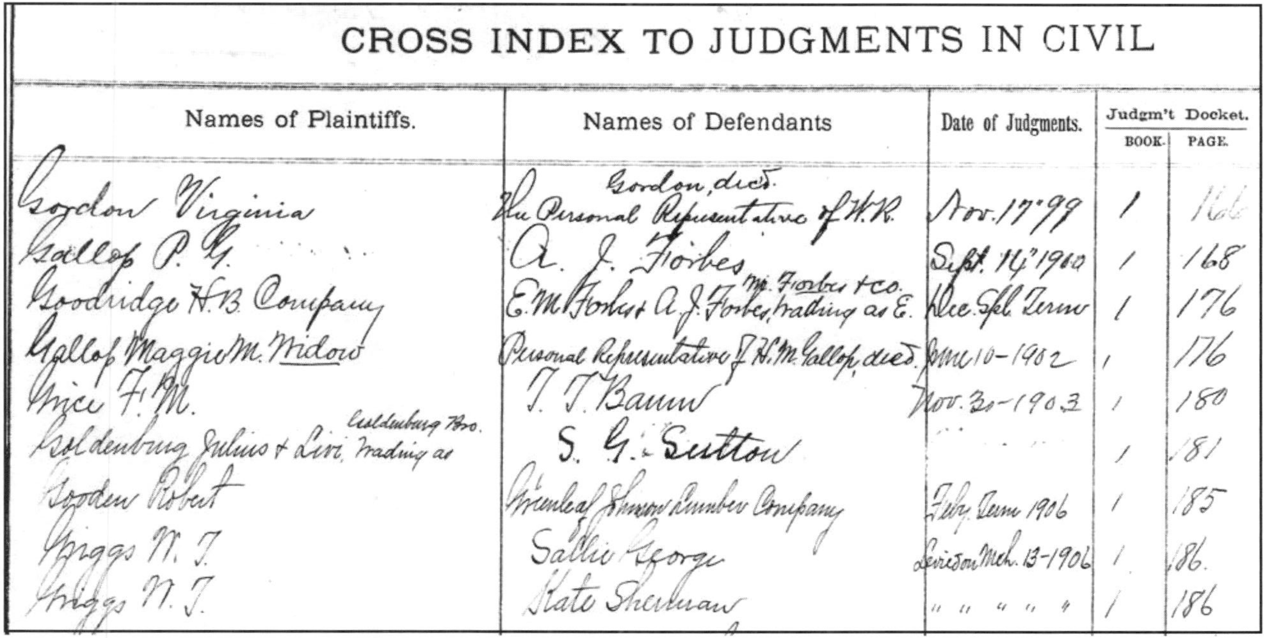

CROSS INDEX TO JUDGMENTS IN CIVIL

Names of Plaintiffs.	Names of Defendants	Date of Judgments.	Judgm't Docket. BOOK.	Judgm't Docket. PAGE.
Gordon Virginia	The Personal Representative of W.R. Gordon, dec'd.	Nov. 17 '99	1	166
Gallop P. G.	A. J. Forbes	Sept. 14 1900	1	168
Goodridge H. B. Company	E. M. Forbes & A. J. Forbes, trading as E. M. Forbes & Co.	Dec. Spl. Term	1	176
Gallop Maggie M. Widow	Personal Representative of H. M. Gallop, dec'd.	June 10-1902	1	176
Grice F. M.	T. T. Bann	Nov. 30-1903	1	180
Goldenburg Julius & Levi, trading as Goldenburg Bro.	S. G. Sutton		1	181
Gooden Robert	Greenleaf Johnson Lumber Company	Feby. Term 1906	1	185
Griggs N. T.	Sallie George	Decision Mch. 13-1906	1	186.
Griggs N. T.	Kate Sherman	" " " " "	1	186

Figure 10-8. A straight-forward Cross Index to Judgments in Civil actions. Plaintiffs are on the left, then defendants' names appear, the date of the judgment, and the Judgment Docket volume and page number. In another section of the index, the defendants were indexed by reversing the columns, defendants on the left, and plaintiffs on the right.

56   COURTHOUSE INDEXES ILLUSTRATED

WILL BOOK

10

HUSTINGS COURT

Figure 10-9. We'll close with the cover of a Hustings Court Will Book index. This court and all its important records are often overlooked. The Hustings Court was found in independent (incorporated) cities which were not a part of the counties they adjoined. This court was particularly seen in Virginia which has a number of independent cities. The Hustings Court was abolished and its duties combined with other courts in the middle of the 20th century but its early records remain and are essential when tracing families. Look for these indexes in the courthouses of independent cities, and watch for them on microfilm listings when using film. The index used within the book illustrated above was similar to other types of indexes illustrated in this present book. The important point to note is to look for Hustings Court indexes while conducting research, if the research is in an independent city. (See Christine Rose, Courthouse Research for Family Historians, *published in San Jose, California by CR Publications in 2004, for a complete list of incorporated cities in Virginia. There are a few others, such as Baltimore, Maryland.)*

INDEX

Bollman's Index, 49-50
Campbell Index, 29-32
    illustration, 30
Cott Indexes, 1-14
    Family Name Index, 6-10
    illustration division by two letters of given name, 11
    groupings by sound, 4
    illustration first two initials, 1
    illustration Grantor Index to Miscellaneous records, 3
    illustration Main Index, 9
    illustration two or three letters of surname, 5
    Main Index, 9-10
    Sub-Index, and illustration of, 6-8
    variations, 10
Cottco Universal Index, 12
    illustrations, 12
Cross Index to Judgments, illustration, 55
Devisee Index, illustration, 40
Devisor/Devisee Index, 39-40
Family Name Indexes, 6-10
    The Main Index, illustration, 9
    The Sub-Index, and illustrations, 6, 7-8
Graves Index, 23-24
    illustration, 24
Hustings Court index cover, illustration, 56
Indexes, Bollman's, 49
    Campbell, 29-31
    Cott, 1-14
    Cross Index to Judgments, 55
    Devisor/Devisee, 39-40
    first initial of given name, 45
    first name variation, 53
    first two letters of surname, 1
    first two or three letters, by sound, 4
    Grantor Index variation, 48
    Graves, 23-24
    Hustings Court, , 56
    Main Index, 9
    Orphan's Court Index, 51, 52
    Proceedings, 25-28
    Russell, 15-22

Indexes, con't., Stark, 37-38
   Sub-Index, 6-8
   three letters of surname, 47
   Town Hall meetings, 53
   Vowel, 33-36
Nicknames, 30
Orphan's Court Index, 51, 52
Proceedings Index, 25-28
   Docket/Index, illustration, 27
   Estate Index, 25
   Estate Index illustration, 26
   illustration of covers, 25
Russell Index, 15-22
   break-out of surnames, 18-19
   illustrations, 17, 18, 21
   in heavily populated areas, 20
   surnames with no key letters, 18
Section number, explanation of, 16
Search procedure in, step-by-step, in Figure 10-2, 45
   in Figure 1-2, 2
   in Figure 1-3, 4
   in Figure 1-4, 6
   in Figure 1-7, 10
   in Figure 2-1 and 2-2, 16, 19
   in Figure 2-3, 20
   in Figure 3-1, 23-24
   in Figure 4-2, 26
   in Figure 5-1, 29-30
   in Figure 6-1, 33-34
   in Figure 7-1, 37
   In Figure 10-4, 49
   in Figure 10-7, 53
Section numbers, explained, 16
Stark Index, and illustration, 37-38
   Sub-Index, illustrations, 7, 8
Town Hall meetings, illustration, 53
Traditional Indexes, 41-44
   Court Order Books, 44
   illustration, 43
   Minute Book, 44
Vowel Index, 33-36
   illustrations, 35-36
   variations, 33